AF571754

STEPHEN MANSFIELD

foreword and original music by AMY GRANT

ZONDERVAN

Welcome Home

Requests for information should be addressed to:

Zondervan, *Grand Rapids, Michigan 49530*

ISBN 978-0-310-51972-0

Cover photo: Sean Murphy/Stone+/Getty Images
Page 34 photo: John F. Phillips/johnphillipsphotography.com
Design: Jody Langley

Printed in the China

10 11 12 13 14 15 • 23 22 21 20 19 18 17 16 15 14 13 12 11 10 9 8 7 6 5 4 3 2 1

TO:
FROM:
DATE:

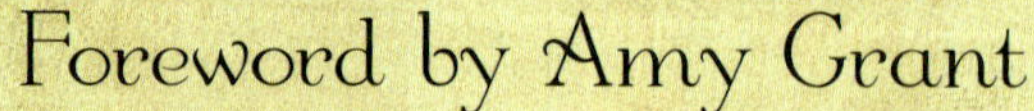

Foreword by Amy Grant

If I tell you my story, and if you listen to me, then I am no longer invisible to you. You will hear my Southern drawl and my slow talking, low voice, and you will know something about my history. In the words that I say, and even in the words that I don't say, you will discover what matters to me. And in discovering my story, you will discover something about yourself, because we are all connected.

If you tell me your story, and if I listen to you, then you are no longer just the kid with the backpack, the woman with the cane, the man in camouflage. Instead, your expressions, your voice, your story become known to me, and I see you differently.

Maybe for the first time, I really see you.

A few years ago I was stuck in a Colorado airport with a crowd of fellow passengers waiting for a delayed flight. I couldn't help but notice a handsome young man in a wheelchair nearby. He was reading the paper, talking on his cell phone, arranging his things. I was captivated by his smile and by the ease with which he managed an extreme disability. He was a triple amputee.

Without asking, I knew he was a veteran. Without knowing his story, I was connected to him.

I own a pair of well-worn, steel-toed combat boots. I wear those boots, but not in the line of duty. They were a gift from the soldier who broke them in, the one who traveled miles of roads in those heavy shoes. Every time I put them on I think about her and I wonder where she is now. We are still connected.

Every day thousands of men and women are serving our country in the military. Every night thousands of families are praying for a safe return. If we knew their names, if we knew their stories, none of us could walk by in silence again.

The stories in this little book represent the stories of these thousands of America's warriors who are coming home from war, who have given their best and who now just want to get back to normal. Hear them. Understand them. Connect to them. Their service is on our behalf. Their sacrifice is for our country. And their return is an opportunity for all of us to say "Welcome Home."

Welcome Home

by Beverly Darnall and Amy Grant

Three weeks after his graduation he
Signed the papers and broke the news
Dad loved his determination, his
Mom and sisters were red, white and blue

Taking his roots and his memories with him
A camouflaged kid in a danger zone
Marks time through the long night watches
Counts on heaven and dreams of home

Thousands of miles away
The family whispers an endless prayer:
Angels of mercy keep him safe 'cause
We need him here, to

welcome home,
welcome home

welcome home,
welcome home

Introduction

by Stephen Mansfield

To Bring Our Valiants Home

We are Americans.
Conceived in a vision of liberty,
And in a faith that longs for a City upon a Hill,

We yearn to live at peace with the nations of the world.
Yet when the strife of men requires
And when the glories of our land are threatened,
We rise to the noble call of arms.

It is then that we send our best,
Our young and our skillful and our fierce,
To stand their watch and slay their foe
And do what a righteous force of arms must do.

And when they are done,
When they have known their weary nights,
Their bloodied hours and their hopeful/fearful days,
When they have left the best they have to offer
On battlefields, now lifetimes away.
We bring them home.

Because we … are Americans.

We brought them home when Washington was done
When Yorktown sang in all our hearts
And our new nation was conceived in blood
And with words that set generations free.

We brought them home from New Orleans,
When General Jackson turned the tide that storied day
And we brought them home from frontiers harsh and lonely
Where they stood guard while our nation found its stride.

And when brother battled brother
In the bloodletting of the blue and the gray,
We brought them home then, too—
The missing leg, the sleeveless jacket—
To homes that healed and spoke of a better day.

Then, after the wars of our friends abroad,
And in struggles that spanned the globe,
We brought our sons and daughters home again
Though we did not always know quite what to do.

In wars on frigid mountains
And after fights in steamy fields,
Our nation, shaken, turned inward
And forgot the debt we owe
The sacred pledge a righteous nation should hold dear.

So we learned
And we healed
And we claimed a sense of honor we had lost.

Because we . . . are Americans.

And now in the dawn of our new millennium
After fights that may seem formless
Against enemies too cowardly to appear,
Again we bring them home.

And this time … we'll do it right!

For we proclaim them heroes
And we welcome our valiants home,
Every selfless one of them,
With tears and hope for honors yet to come.

So laud them, sing their courage to the sky
And tell a people yet unborn
Of their valor and their grace.

For these … are our returning heroes.
And we know what we might be
Had they not gone, not stood their watch.
Not held our enemies at bay.

We welcome them—home.

To Stand for Those Who Stayed

WHEN MAJOR DAN ROONEY BOARDED United Airlines flight 664 on that wet, nasty night at Chicago's O'Hare Airport, he noticed the young corporal in his dress Army greens sitting in first class. It pleased him to think that some kind passenger had given up his seat for this soldier, for it had been a miserable night of travel for everyone.

There had been storms and delays. Rooney was making his way from Grand Haven, Michigan, where he co-owned Grand Haven Golf Club with his father, and was trying to reach Grand Rapids. The layover at Chicago had been long and frustrating and now it was nearly midnight. Rooney was weary, as were all the passengers, but he was glad to see someone had taken care of that young warrior up in first class.

The plane finally landed in Grand Rapids at nearly twelve-thirty in the morning, but it was then that the captain made an announcement. "Ladies and gentleman," he began soberly, "Tonight we have an American hero on board." Dan Rooney thought this must surely be the young man he had seen before. The captain continued: "We are carrying the remains of Brock Bucklin, twenty-eight years old. His twin brother, Brad, has accompanied his body the 6000 miles from Iraq. I want to ask everyone to remain seated until the coffin is removed from the plane and the honor guard you see out your window has completed its task. Thank you."

It was then that Rooney understood. The young soldier in first class wasn't there because of a kind passenger. He was there because United Airlines was trying to make his journey easier, because they knew that the body down below was this young man's twin brother. And now his grieving family was about to welcome their dead son home.

Rooney sat nearly at attention in seat 24A, slowly feeling the sadness of the moment wash over him. He was not a man unacquainted with war. He belonged to the Oklahoma Air National Guard and had already done three tours in Iraq flying F16s. It had been his privilege to provide close air support for troops on the ground and though he saw with each tour that the situation was improving, he also knew that the sands of Iraq were stained with the blood of great patriots. He knew it, but had not seen it, and now from the window of this United jet he was about to experience war from the other side.

As he watched, rain fell on a flag-draped coffin. The Bucklin family wept when they saw it. Corporal Brad Bucklin tried to keep his military bearing but it was his twin brother who was in that coffin and now he had to present his parents with their dead child. There were tears and hugs and rain-soaked salutes. Then Rooney saw Brock Bucklin's four year-old son. He was weeping and screaming. Wearied by grief, he collapsed on the wet tarmac. It was almost more than the Major could bear.

He was soon distracted from the scene, though. He had noticed that the passengers sat still at first, as the captain had requested. But ten or fifteen minutes later, some of the passengers got up and walked off the plane. Others followed. Soon, nearly half had left and Rooney felt a deep anger joining the sadness that filled his heart. He looked from the gut wrenching scene out his window to the sight of passengers collecting their luggage and walking away, chattering their uncaring nonsense as they went. And Rooney grew angrier still, but before long his anger showed him what he must do.

As soon as the ceremony was done and Rooney was off the plane, he called his wife. It was the wee hours of the morning but she had to know what had happened and what he had decided to do. “I have a different mission in life now,” he told her. “I’m sure a higher power is guiding me.”

Rooney had decided he must help the children of America’s fallen warriors. He had to help take care of the thousands of little children like the son of Brock Bucklin whom he had seen on that tarmac. He also knew that his connection to professional golf provided the key. He had long been proud of the fact that the nation’s Professional Golf Association (PGA) courses contributed more to charity than professional football, basketball, and baseball combined. This was how Dan Rooney would change the lives of those fallen warrior’s children.

So Rooney created Patriot Day and with the help of the PGA he has made it a national effort. Every year, PGA golf courses around the country designate Labor Day weekend as a time when golfers can add a dollar to their green fees to support scholarships for the children of those killed in war. Generous, patriotic golfers have embraced the idea and in 2008 some four thousand PGA golf courses raised more than two million dollars for scholarships. Rooney dreams of even more and already a building is being constructed purely through donations and new golf courses are joining the efforts with each passing month.

For Rooney, though, the greatest payoff is in the faces of the children of America's fallen whose lives are changed by the scholarships Patriot Day provides. And Rooney will never forget the first scholarship the program ever gave, for it was to Jacob Bucklin, the son of Brock Bucklin, the warrior whose body was put on Rooney's plane that wet Chicago night.

Now, while he continues to fly F16s and while he continues to run a golf course with his father, Major Dan Rooney also travels the country as a champion of Patriot Day. As he does, he tells his audiences that he wants them to do something special. He wants them to take a stand for the passengers on United flight 664 who stayed behind and showed respect. He wants them to welcome America's fallen with honor.

www.foldsofhonor.org and www.patriotgolfday.com

Currahee

IT WAS WHAT BRIAN BRENNAN WANTED TO DO. It was what he had dreamed of since he was a boy, why he had attended The Citadel—The Military College of South Carolina—and why he had been so eager to be commissioned into the Army in 2006. He wanted to be an Airborne Ranger. He wanted to be among the elite and the feared. And when he was assigned to the 101st Airborne and found himself in the 506th Infantry Regiment, he was both humbled and thrilled. This was the famous "Band of Brothers" regiment, the one that had distinguished itself during World War II and which had been so celebrated in literature and film. This was where he belonged, why he had trained, and who he wanted to be.

He was feeling his place in history, then, on that day in May of 2008 when he was riding in a Humvee through Zanbar, Afghanistan. His assignment was to analyze the area and find ways to improve the quality of life for Afghan civilians. He loved the work, thought it noble, and felt it was in the best of the Ranger tradition.

On that particular day in May, though, he had something else on his mind. He had just rolled into an area behind the market and he recalls thinking that it was too quiet, that the area was too empty, which usually meant that insurgents were about. It was the last thought he can remember. Suddenly, his Humvee hit an IED—an improvised explosive device—killing all aboard but Brennan and his driver.

Lt. Brennan would remember very little of the following months. The blast of that IED took both his legs, damaged his arms and left him in a coma. Flown back to Walter Reed Army Medical Center in Washington D.C., he lay in a nearly vegetative state, his eyes open but vacant, seeing nothing. His mother longed for "those beautiful blue eyes" to come alive and see her loving face once again, but it was not likely to be. Doctors told Brennan's parents to prepare for the possibility that there might never be a change.

Two weeks after Brian was hit, while he lay unaware in his hospital bed, General David Petraeus visited Walter Reed, accompanied by Command Sergeant Major Marvin Hill. They toured the wounded as was their habit when the General was in town, speaking the encouraging word and sharing the laugh or two with recovering men and women. As the tour neared its end, the men found themselves at the bed of Brian Brennan. They were told how bad it was and how there had been no response, how devastating it had all been for the family.

For a moment Petraeus and Hill were without words. They felt deep affinity for this man. He was Airborne, after all, and the General and the Command Sergeant Major had led the 101st during the first years in Iraq. And they were proud of it. In fact, CSM Hill had a reputation for refusing to wear a coat in cold weather because it would mean covering up the Screaming Eagles on his uniform. What was a bit of chill compared to unit pride? So both men felt what a band of brothers feels for its wounded, that love shared by "The Brotherhood of the Close Fight."

They tried their best to awaken Brennan. They had done this kind of thing before. General Petraeus shouted "Air Assault, Lieutenant!" to try to bring the Ranger to consciousness. There was nothing. Then they spoke softly. "We're proud of you, big guy. Thanks for all you've been through, and thanks for the leadership you provided to your troopers." And so it went, but Lt. Brennan did not stir.

Finally, it was time to go but Petraeus wasn't finished. He had decided to make one last attempt and suddenly shouted "Currahee!" The knowing in the room smiled. It was the nickname of the 506th, the Cherokee word which means "We stand alone." It was the Ranger shout of encouragement to fellow Rangers. And it was heritage. Men training at Camp Toccoa in Georgia during World War II would have trained on Mount Currahee and would have had that word burned into their souls nearly every day of their careers. Every Ranger knew it, tried to live it, and was inspired by it.

Including Lt. Brian Brennan. When General Petraeus shouted that honored word, he thought he saw Brennan respond. Petraeus whispered to CSM Hill, "Did you see something?" Hill thought he had but wasn't sure: "I don't know, sir, but let's give it another try." And so on the count of three, the two men shouted, "Currahee!" And then it happened. Brennan began to react. His head moved back and forth. His stumps beat wildly on the sheets. His eyes seemed to focus a bit. Everyone in the room could see that he had heard that Ranger call.

And while tears filled their eyes, Petraeus and Hill watched Lt. Brian Brennan begin his journey out of the darkness and back to conscious life.

It would take months and it would never be easy, but Brennan made a recovery that doctors called miraculous. His mind cleared. He found his voice again. His body strengthened. In time, he began training on his new prosthetics to run marathons. And though he cannot remember that day at Walter Reed, he has no problem believing that the word Currahee did the trick. It was buried in the back of his mind, he says, and when others called it out, that word—and that summons to brotherhood—roared him back to consciousness. Brennan, who reveres the Ranger tradition, is not surprised.

Nor are Brennan's friends and family surprised that he has decided to stay in the Army and serve wounded soldiers like himself. There is a foundation in his name now and he wants to use it to help restore those ravaged in battle. And he knows he can make a difference: "Everyone who goes into war knows what can happen. Some get hurt, some don't. Live with your opportunities to the fullest for the guys who don't come back. If you have injuries, don't let it hold you back. Just keep driving on."

And so Brian Brennan has.

Currahee!

www.brennanstandsalone.org

No Longer an Outcast

CHRISTOPHER TRITICO WAS STANDING in a Marine Corps recruiting office on September 11, 2001. He had already planned to join the Marines before that terrible day began and he ended up watching America's humiliation play out on a recruiter's television. He was angry and wanted to fight back. But he was also young and easily distracted, he says, so he dragged his feet. Finally, in 2005, he signed up and completed his basic training at Camp Lejeune. This is how he found himself in Fallujah, Iraq, in 2006 with the 36th Marine Corps Infantry Division.

He was soon thrust into the now famous fight for that city, but what he remembers most is the kindness of the civilians there. They frequently offered food to Tritico and his buddies, and the Marines almost always gratefully accepted before they realized that these big-hearted Iraqis were giving all they had. The Marines answered this generosity with beef jerky and protein bars and it wasn't long before understanding set in, and then friendship.

Still, Corporal Tritico saw horrible things. There was that day he was doing security on the roof of a building and he noticed a patrol walking to the far end of a square. Suddenly, there was a massive explosion. Lance Corporal Rosa—a jokester, the guy everyone liked and wanted to be around—had stepped on an IED. He was dead and so was most of his patrol. Tritico was devastated. Morale suffered horribly in his unit for months after.

Then there was the time he was on radio watch with a fellow Marine. The two men talked for hours. They discussed their girlfriends back home and their plans for the future and even their thinking about the war. When their shift was over, they said goodbye and went their separate ways. Moments later, there was a commotion. Someone hurrying by said that the Marine Tritico had just spent hours talking to was dead. He was dropped by sniper fire or maybe by a stray bullet that hit him in the neck. Tritico never knew for sure and didn't get to see his friend's body before it was evacuated, but having talked so openly with the man in the last hours of his life left Tritico feeling sick and depressed.

All of this fed into the night when Corporal Tritico was lying in bed and an explosion knocked him to the floor He ran outside with other Marines, most still in their standard issue green pajamas. A huge bomb had exploded and dozens had been killed. Soon trucks began bringing the civilian dead and Tritico was put to work unloading the bodies. He will never forget it. Most were dead but some were still alive and they fixed their eyes on him and groaned out their last words. But he didn't understand, couldn't offer comfort. Nearly all who spoke to him eventually died. The idea of men saying the last words they would ever speak in this world to a man who couldn't understand tortured Tritico. He thought of it often—the bloodied faces and the eyes fixed upon him and the words offered in vain as death approached.

Then months passed and it was time to go home. He remembers thinking how strange it would be after what he had been through. And he remembers the flight to Cherry Point, the Marine Corps Air Station in North Carolina. And he remembers the excitement of that bus ride to the parking lot at Camp Lejeune.

Waiting in that parking lot, Sam Tritico, Christopher's dad, somehow knew that his son was on that third bus and he got as close as he could. Parents were not allowed to cross that yellow line, though. The officials at Camp Lejeune had already made this clear. So Sam had to hold himself in check, had to wait just a few minutes longer to put his arms around his boy. But then the buses came to a stop, the doors opened, and Corporal Christopher Tritico was the first one off that third bus. And Sam, his father, ran to him in tears and relief.

Corporal Christopher Tritico remembers that moment in the Camp Lejeune parking lot when he threw himself into his father's arms and then hugged the rest of his family, including his beautiful fiancé. He was home and he was loved. They were all heading to the beach for a vacation and it was going to be wonderful. He noticed, though, that there were Marines who had no one to greet them and this left him depressed. He also took a last tearful look at the makeshift memorial to the seven comrades his unit had lost. Their faces would never leave him, he determined. He would honor them by how he lived.

It was good to have Christopher home. Sam noticed that his son was thinner but he was healthy and his workouts while overseas had given him a body of steel. He also noticed that Christopher had aged, that there was something in his face that comes from suffering and grief. Sam was relieved, then, that Christopher seemed to have his old sense of humor, that he still told jokes and loved to play with children and still brandished his trademark razor wit.

Sam knew things weren't quite right, though. Christopher had never been an observant man and this meant he had never been a very good driver or much in tune with what was going on around him. He seemed always in his own little world. Now, Christopher was hyper-observant. Sam would drive down the road with his son in the car and Christopher would jolt suddenly and say, "Dad, watch out! There's a ..."

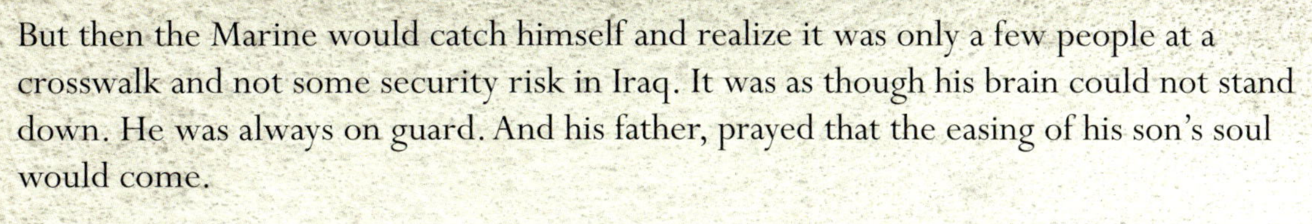

But then the Marine would catch himself and realize it was only a few people at a crosswalk and not some security risk in Iraq. It was as though his brain could not stand down. He was always on guard. And his father, prayed that the easing of his son's soul would come.

Being home was a chaotic experience for Christopher. Everything seemed to be in motion, moving too fast. It was hard to explain to his folks that in Iraq there were times of urgency and violence, of course, but often there were days on end that were quiet, almost peaceful. Life, even at war, moved at a slower pace. By contrast, the U.S. was a confusing swirl.

He was also dogged by the tension he felt everywhere he went. Walking into a Walmart, he automatically looked for snipers on the roof. He scanned sidewalks for the wires of explosives and watched crowds for signs of an ambush. He couldn't keep himself from thinking that every bag of trash on the side of the road was a bomb, every bumpy patch of blacktop an IED.

He was always on guard whether he wanted to be or not. If a few women in a grocery store accidentally hemmed him in with their shopping carts, he felt threatened and aggressively pushed the carts out of the way. In restaurants he sat where he could quickly escape, always preferring a booth with no one behind him. He was unconsciously planning for disaster all the time and he could not make it stop.

Then there was the fear. He felt it without cause and without warning. One night he woke up in a hotel room convinced he had lost his rifle. He ran around the room looking for it, sure his commanders would be enraged. Then, suddenly, he caught himself—and wondered about the tricks his mind could play.

Always, he knew his family loved him but he could not make them understand. He showed them pictures from his days in Iraq but he knew they did not feel what he did about what they saw. He couldn't blame them. He hardly knew what to feel himself. He decided to let it go and use his humor to build a bridge. Even this failed him. His gift for comedy had been transformed by war. He would tell a joke but it fell flat. He would try to tease but it would only confuse.

He was feeling what nearly all of his comrades from Iraq felt. There was the tension and the fear but also the emotion of losing friends. There was the imprint of the unspeakable violence upon his soul and there were the uncertain memories that came from his time in Iraq being both the best and the worst of his life.

He knew he had what they call post-traumatic stress disorder. Every warrior he knew had it too. They were all tempted to sit in a dark room and drink, all tempted to disconnect from life back home to live in the lifeless shadow of Iraq.

But Christopher Tritico decided not to give in. He decided he was going to beat this thing. Hours of thought and reflection had made him certain of his reasons why.

First, there was his family. They were trying so hard. They made clumsy attempts to reach him and sometimes they were a pain. But they stayed close, showed him they wanted to be in his life and wouldn't let go. They were always inviting him out—to a game or to go surfing or to just hang out over some food—and the fact that they wouldn't pull back kept him engaged. "Me trying to be normal for them made me normal," he recalls.

His faith also held him fast. He believes in God and believes that there was a purpose for his life. He had seen horrendous things, yes, but these weren't outside of God's ability to heal and they didn't change the divine plan for his life. So Christopher clung

to his purpose and prayed that God would do whatever had to be done to make him ready to play his role on earth. And God began to restore him, Christopher says.

Always there were his dreams. He had married that gorgeous fiancé and they had things they wanted to do. He would not let her down. He had also been in a rock band once and he was pretty good. Who knew where his music might lead. He even thought that one day he might own a health club where he could teach people what he had learned about physical fitness, about surviving and about rising above the hard things of life. No, his dreams were too valuable to let Iraq steal them away. Christopher Tritico was going to live the life of his hopes.

So on the strength of his family, his faith and his dreams, Corporal Tritico has come home. Not just in body but in mind and heart. It wasn't easy and there was many a troubled night. But he is back, now, and ready to take his life in hand. And a grateful nation hopes that all her warrior sons and daughters will find what Christopher Tritico has found.

For Who He Was At Heart

There is a Swahili warrior's proverb that says:

Life has meaning only in the struggle,

Victory or defeat is in the hand of God.

So let us celebrate the struggle.

These words resonate with Sergeant Joey Bozik. "I don't want to risk not struggling," he says. "Struggles make you stronger. People always ask, 'Why? Why me? Why did this have to happen?' You can't look at it that way. Struggle is a positive thing. It teaches you lessons and makes you stronger. Where would we be without the struggles in our lives?"

Bozik speaks from a depth of experience with hardship and suffering that most men will never know. This began on an October day in 2004 as Bozik was serving in the 118th Military Police Company (Airborne) sixty miles south of Baghdad. He was only 26 but he had already provided security in Bosnia, at the Pentagon for nine months after September 11, 2001, and in Afghanistan. Now he was in Iraq, and on October 27 he received a call from a Marine unit that they had discovered an IED and needed protection until the EOD—the Explosive Ordinance Detail—arrived.

Bozik and his two men mounted their Humvee and drove immediately to where those Marines were, but as they turned down the side of an overpass as part of a three vehicle convoy, their front right tire—near where Bozik sat—rolled over an IED. His body absorbed most of the blast, which tore off both of his legs and his right arm.

Two weeks later, he found himself at Walter Reed Army Hospital trying to clear his head and understand what had happened to him. He listened as doctors explained what his future might be, as psychologists tried to help him adapt and as his family drew around him with comfort and care. As the reality of his situation set in, Joey appreciated all of those who tried to help him, but he quickly realized what he had to do.

That was when he asked to be alone with Jayme.

He had been pretty sure she was the one. They had met when a fellow soldier in Afghanistan told Bozik that he talked just like a girl he knew back home. The two had emailed each other, spoken a bit by phone, and then finally met when he was on leave. They had grown close and Jayme had said that she didn't want to see anyone else, that she thought what they had was special. She would wait for him to return. They talked about their future together and they even pondered what it would mean if he was wounded in the war.

Now, finding himself a triple amputee in a bed at Walter Reed, Bozik wanted to set Jayme free. "I told her I would completely understand if she wanted to walk away," he remembers. "I said I wouldn't hold it against her at all. I just needed to know right then and there, while I was all busted up. I didn't want to go through the heartache later. I had seen other men recovering in that hospital whose wives and children had abandoned them because they just couldn't take it. There those men lay all lonely and broken. I wanted Jayme to know she could go but I wanted her to do it right then. Not two or three years later when I had come to rely on her, when she found it all to be too much. After all, everyone has dreams of what their life is going to be like. They picture being on the beach or skiing or skydiving and they want to do those things with their spouse. But I couldn't and I needed Jayme to decide if she could handle it."

It turned out that Ms. Jayme Peters was made of tougher stuff than some of the women Bozik had seen. She said she didn't want to leave. "I don't want to be with anyone else," she told him. "You still have a heart and you still have a mind and that's all I need."

"Well," Joey Bozik said, "I guess we're getting married then."

His next conversation was with Jayme's father. Over the phone, he asked Mr. Peters if he had permission to marry his daughter. "Nothing would make me prouder," came the kind reply.

So it was that on December 31, 2004—just eight weeks after he was almost killed in Iraq—Sergeant Joey Bozik married Jayme Peters in the chapel at Walter Reed. There were family members present and even some "hospital brass"—senior officers Joey had come to know—and he remembers that it was the first time since his injuries that he had been out of bed. He got married in a wheelchair, in uniform and to the radiant bride he loved.

The marriage since then has been sweet, Joey says. The love of a good woman changes everything and then there is Violet, their daughter, who is their delight.

But always there are the struggles. There was the difficult decision to endure a second amputation on one of his legs because the prosthesis wouldn't work right given the damage to his knee. Then Joey had to learn how to be married and how to be a banker at Wells Fargo. Always, too, he battled the haunting thoughts that came from his injuries and the war.

But Joey Bozik is willing to take it all on, willing to risk the struggles of his life. Because he is loved by Jayme, a woman of strength and iron will. Because he wants to honor the Purple Heart that hangs upon his chest. And because he knows his struggles will help make him the man he wants to be.

www.challengeamerica.com

Gone The Days of Dishonor

WHEN DAN MCKINNEY RETURNED from the Vietnam War in 1970, he was met at Dallas' Love Field airport by a crowd yelling obscenities at him simply because he was in the Army. He had returned to a nation tearing itself apart, to a people seemingly at war with themselves over nearly every issue. Soldiers, who had only done their best to serve their country in Vietnam, were now called "baby-killers," "terrorists," the "storm-troopers" of President Nixon's "fascist regime." The wounds of that era seemed that they would never heal.

These memories must surely have played in McKinney's mind when nearly thirty-five years later he was summoned once again by his country and once again to a war in a far off place. His regular job for decades had been with the Bureau of Customs and Border Protection in Miami, but he was also a Sergeant in the Third Battalion, 247th Regiment, of the Army Reserves. He was not surprised that he was needed in Iraq since he was an expert K-9 handler and an experienced law enforcement officer with experience at war. Iraqi police officers were beginning to keep order in their emerging democracy and Dan McKinney was just the kind of man to show them how.

This is what put him in that dining facility at a U.S. compound in Iraq. Sergeant First Class Dan McKinney had just given his Iraqi police students a lunch break and had just sat down with his meal. It was quiet. The door to the facility opened, which made McKinney look up. It was just a lieutenant coming in for a meal. McKinney returned to his food, and that is when a suicide bomber stepped through the same door and blew himself up. The lieutenant and two of McKinney's Iraqi students were instantly killed. Eighteen others were wounded. McKinney knew immediately he'd been hit but he heard a soldier moaning behind him. Thinking there might be a second explosion, he picked up this wounded man and took him to safety through a gaping hole in a wall.

He was just heading back into the decimated dining facility to find more wounded men when some soldiers saw how badly he was hurt and took him to a casualty point nearby. As medics began treating him, McKinney lapsed into unconsciousness and then fell into a coma. For four days doctors tried to revive him. Finally, he came to at Walter Reed Army Medical Center. He was alive, but he had a wound to his abdomen that would take nearly a year and a half to heal.

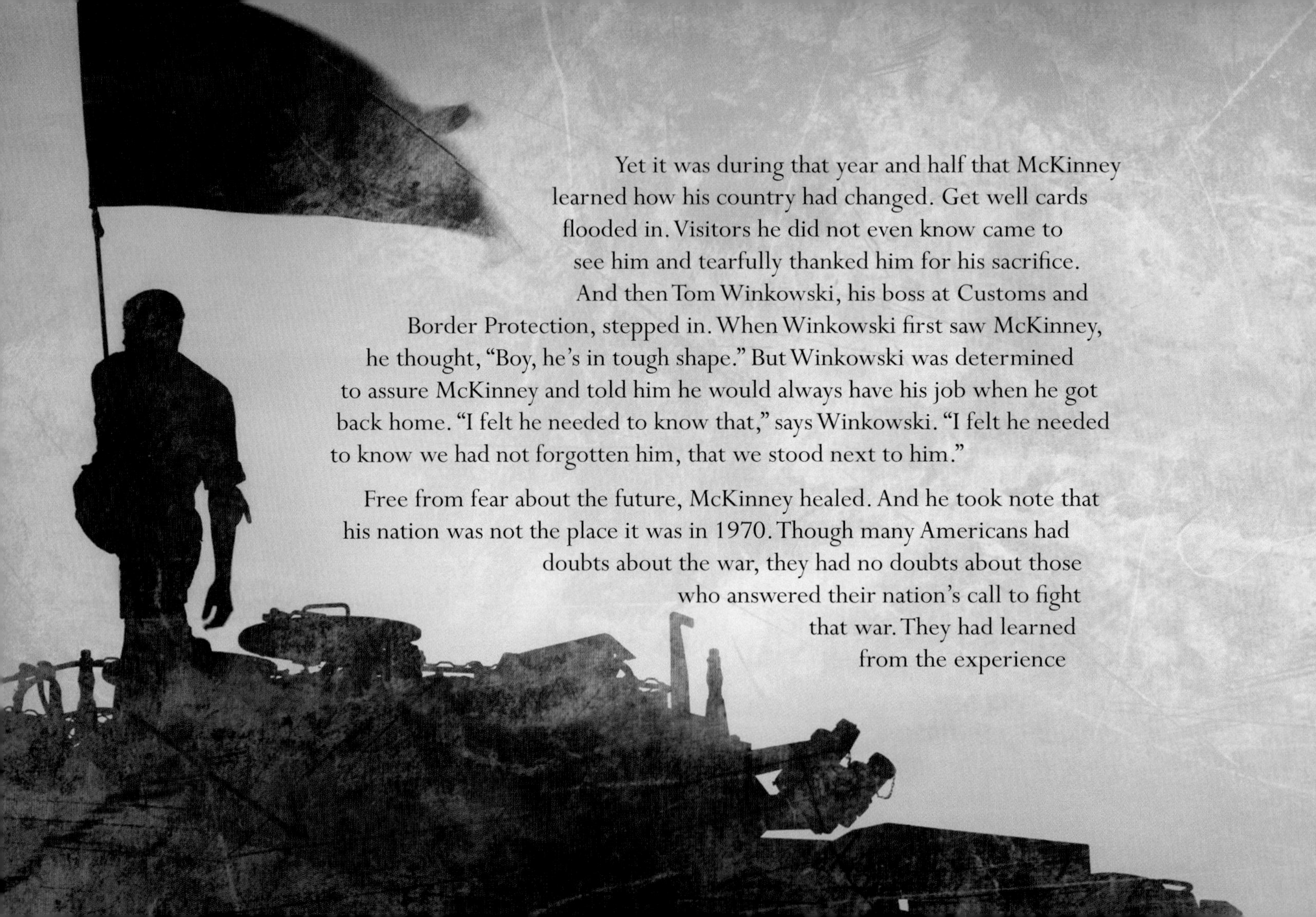

Yet it was during that year and half that McKinney learned how his country had changed. Get well cards flooded in. Visitors he did not even know came to see him and tearfully thanked him for his sacrifice. And then Tom Winkowski, his boss at Customs and Border Protection, stepped in. When Winkowski first saw McKinney, he thought, "Boy, he's in tough shape." But Winkowski was determined to assure McKinney and told him he would always have his job when he got back home. "I felt he needed to know that," says Winkowski. "I felt he needed to know we had not forgotten him, that we stood next to him."

Free from fear about the future, McKinney healed. And he took note that his nation was not the place it was in 1970. Though many Americans had doubts about the war, they had no doubts about those who answered their nation's call to fight that war. They had learned from the experience of Vietnam and now knew that they could love the soldier even if they hated the war. McKinney was relieved to know this, to see that his countrymen treated him with kindness and respect. He knew his nation honored what he had endured. It helped him heal from wounds both of body and of soul.

While he did, he had a special visitor to his hospital room. It was the soldier whom he had carried to safety after that explosion in Iraq. The young man brought his family to McKinney's room and they all told him what he meant to them and how they would never forget.

On January 22, 2007, Sergeant First Class Dan McKinney returned to work at the Bureau of Customs and Border Protection. There was applause from his fellow workers and pats on the back. And Dan McKinney was welcomed home, once again—this time as a warrior should be.

Honor For A Georgia Son

THEY WERE JUST A FEW LINES in a small town newspaper. A local man, Sergeant First Class John C. Beale, had been killed in Afghanistan. His body would arrive at Falcon Field in Fayette County, Georgia, the next day—June 11, 2009. The Henry Country Police Department would escort the hearse to the funeral home several counties over. And then there were the lines that everyone remembered: "We are asking all those who are able to line the streets along the route to help honor this fallen hero and give him the welcome he deserves. Please share this information with your friends and family."

It would usually not be worth mentioning. Beale was a fallen hero, true, and he had even served in the first Gulf War, the one they called Desert Storm, back some fifteen years ago. Otherwise, his story was pretty normal. He had gone to Riverdale High School and then worked for the Clayton Country Water Authority. His father had been a sailor and this heritage made him love the military, made him want to join the National Guard. He attended Eagle's Landing First Baptist Church and devoted himself to Crystal, his wife, and their two children, Christopher and Calye.

That was it: an average man from a small town in Georgia who had given his life for his country. In some places in America, it would hardly be worth mentioning.

But this was Georgia and in Georgia soldiers don't die without people saying thank you, without folks taking a moment to remember and reflect.

The hearse pulled out of the Falcon Field Airport parking lot, a little after six that June evening. The journey to the funeral home would take nearly a half an hour. Some folks wouldn't have believed what happened next if a state trooper hadn't turned on his video camera to record the entire journey.

They came. First by the hundreds and then by the thousands, they left their homes and their businesses and they took their children in hand and they stood their post along the route that took John Beale's body home. All along that 25 miles there were families waving flags and veterans at salute and entire National Guard units standing at attention. There were miles of just average people who had no reason to be there except that they had read the lines in the paper and knew what an

American must do. So they made sure they were there. In wheelchairs; with canes; on daddy's shoulders; Sunday school classes and book clubs. They turned out and stood there—many with tears in their eyes and their hands on their hearts—to tell John Beale what he meant to a grateful people.

It was astonishing. From Falcon Field through Stuarts Mill, on through Fayette County to Lovejoy and then, finally, to Henry County, the procession slowly wound, with flags and firemen and farmers and Boy Scouts lining the way. Eighty people at an intersection there, two hundred in that bank parking lot there. All bowed their heads and knew that respect for America's fallen was not dead that day.

The state trooper's video made it onto YouTube and millions saw how John Beale was honored. They saw that the way it was on a June day in Georgia was the way America should be.

Now John Beale's body rests at the Camp Memorial Cemetery in Fayetteville, Georgia. He has been welcomed home, and his homecoming has ignited a holy pride and patriotism that our country is richer for recovering. Rest well, John Beale. Welcome home.

Music
ZONDERVAN
Welcome Home
STEPHEN MANSFIELD
forward and original music by AMY GRANT